9/12

We Love Holidays

Celebrating Yom Kippur

Honor Head

PowerKiDS
press.
New York

Published in 2009 by The Rosen Publishing Group Inc.
29 East 21st Street, New York, NY 10010

First Edition

Series Editor: Jean Coppendale
Senior Design Manager: Simmi Sikka
Designer: Sheeba Narain

Library of Congress Cataloging-in-Publication Data

Head, Honor.
  Celebrating Yom Kippur / Honor Head. – 1st ed.
     p. cm. – (We love holidays)
  Includes index.
  ISBN 978-1-4358-2846-9 (library binding)
  ISBN 978-1-4358-2906-0 (paperback)
  ISBN 978-1-4358-2910-7 (6-pack)
  1. Yom Kippur–Juvenile literature. I. Title.
  BM695.A8H43 2009
  296.4'32–dc22
                              2008030330

Manufactured in China

The publishers would like to thank the following for allowing us to reproduce
their pictures in this book:
Shutterstock: title, 9 Lisa F. Young / Alamy: 4, Profimedia International s.r.o. /
REUTERS: 5, Michael Dalder; 23, Havakuk Levison / CORBIS: 6, PoodlesRock;
7, Bettmann; 11, Ted Spiegel; 12, Steve Raymer; 14, Philippe Lissac/Godong; 15,
David Rubinger; 17, Karen Huntt / Photolibrary: 8, Foodpix; cover, 13, 19, Photo
Researchers, Inc.; 16, The Bridgeman Art Library / Lily & Rob: 10 / Ark Religion: 18,
Helene Rogers / Shutterstock: 20, Blaz Kure / Judy Lash Balint: 21 / Sigalit Perkol: 22.

Contents

Web Sites
Due to the changing nature of Internet links, PowerKids Press has developed an online list of Web sites related to the subject of this book. This site is updated regularly. Please use this link to access this list: www.powerkidslinks.com/wlh/yomkip

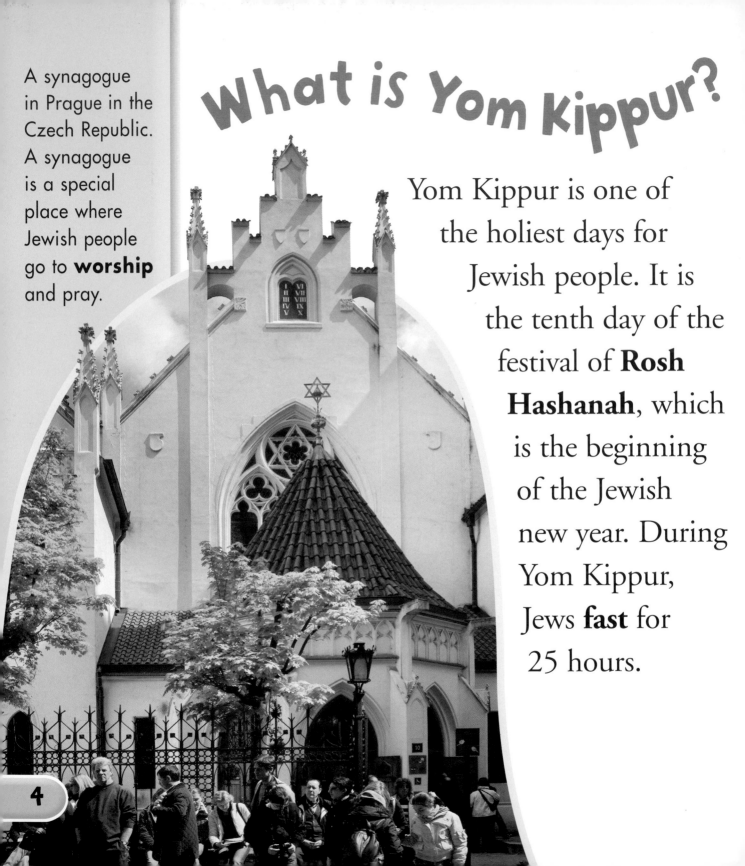

What is Yom Kippur?

A synagogue in Prague in the Czech Republic. A synagogue is a special place where Jewish people go to **worship** and pray.

Yom Kippur is one of the holiest days for Jewish people. It is the tenth day of the festival of **Rosh Hashanah**, which is the beginning of the Jewish new year. During Yom Kippur, Jews **fast** for 25 hours.

Many Jews spend the day of Yom Kippur in the synagogue. They pray and ask God for forgiveness for all the wrong things they have done. They also remember how much God loves them.

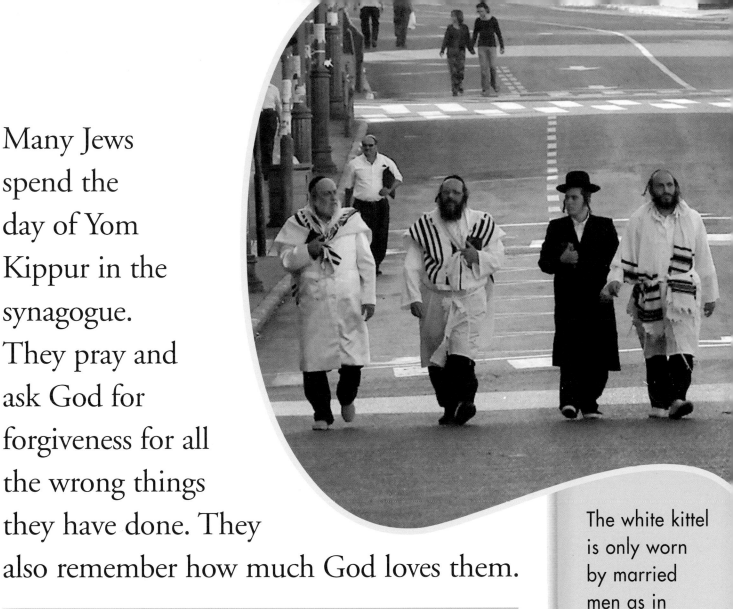

The white kittel is only worn by married men as in this picture.

DID YOU KNOW?

On special occasions, such as Yom Kippur, many Jewish men wear a white garment called a kittel, which stands for pure thoughts.

Moses and the golden calf

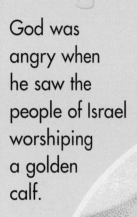

God was angry when he saw the people of Israel worshiping a golden calf.

Yom Kippur started in **ancient** times with the **prophet** Moses. He found the people of Israel worshiping a statue of a golden calf instead of God. Moses pleaded with God to forgive them.

The people also asked God for forgiveness and fasted from sunset to sunrise. God forgave them, and Moses said that from that day onward, on the tenth day of the seventh month, the people of Israel would fast and ask God for forgiveness for their sins.

Moses went to the top of Mount Sinai and asked God to forgive the people of Israel.

The eve of Yom Kippur

Kreplach are small parcels of pasta filled with minced meat.

On the evening before Yom Kippur, many Jewish families pray to God. Then they have their last meal before they fast. The meal may include chicken soup with kreplach.

8

The meal may also include a bread called challah. This is a **traditional** Jewish bread, which is eaten on most holidays and festivals.

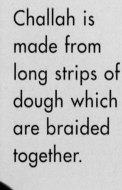

Challah is made from long strips of dough which are braided together.

special blessings

Also on the eve on Yom Kippur, two special candles are lit to remember parents who have died. The candles are left to burn throughout the day.

The family light two candles at the start of Yom Kippur.

10

Before they leave for the synagogue, many parents say a **blessing** for their children. The parents ask God to look after their children and keep them safe.

Many Jewish parents say sorry for the times they may have upset their children during the year.

At the synagogue

The first prayer said at the start of the first evening service in the synagogue is called Kol Nidre. This is when Jews ask for forgiveness for promises they have not kept during the past year.

The men wear a tallitot, or prayer shawl, to say Kol Nidre.

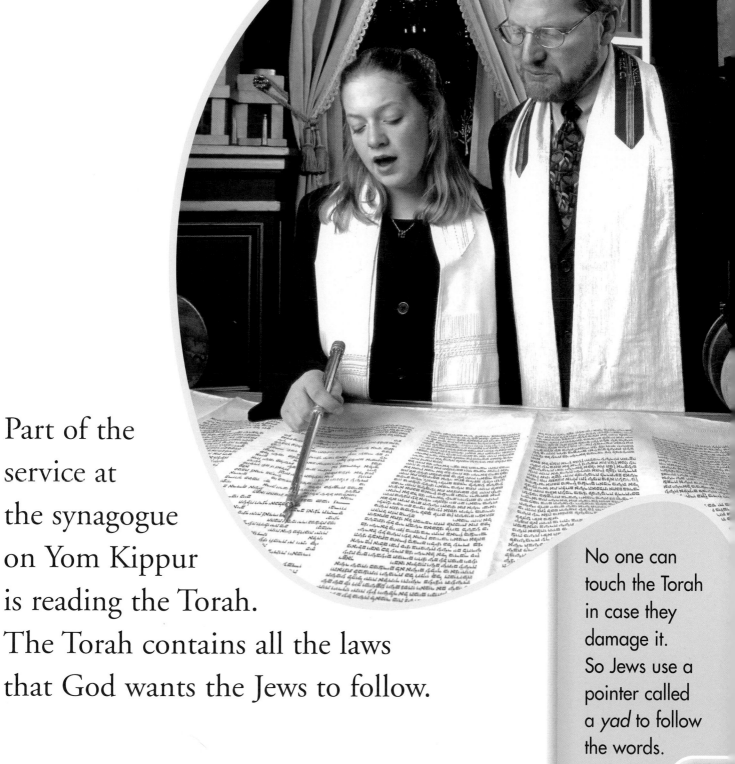

Part of the
service at
the synagogue
on Yom Kippur
is reading the Torah.
The Torah contains all the laws
that God wants the Jews to follow.

No one can
touch the Torah
in case they
damage it.
So Jews use a
pointer called
a *yad* to follow
the words.

Prayers for forgiveness

An important part of Yom Kippur is Avodah. This is a special service when Jews say a series of prayers to God to ask for his forgiveness.

The inside of a synagogue is brightly lit during services.

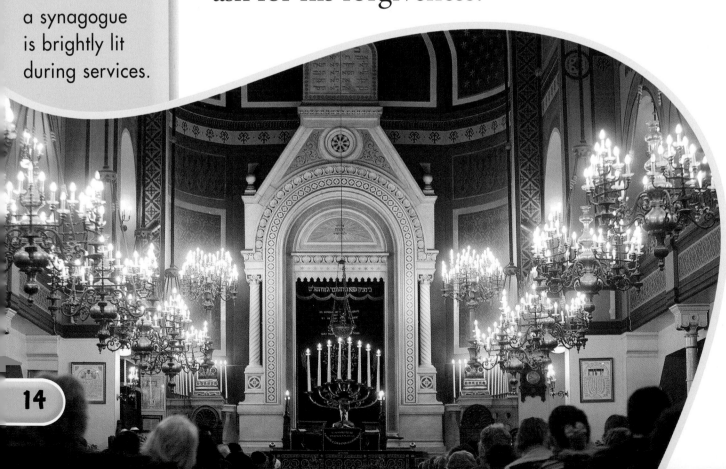

The **rabbi** leads the Avodah prayers. The first prayer is called Hineini, which means "Here I am." It reminds Jews that they have all done wrong things and all need forgiveness, even the person leading the prayers.

A *rabbi* is a Jewish leader. This rabbi is taking the special Avodah service in a synagogue in Israel.

15

Jonah and the whale

This picture is from a Jewish Bible. It shows that God sent a whale to save Jonah from drowning when he fell into the sea.

תבוא מה ארץ
ויאמר אליהן
אלהי השמי
את הים ואת
יראה גדולה ו
יעשית כי ידע
יהוה הוא כי
אלין מה מנש
מי לינו כי הי
אליהם שאו

In the afternoon, the story of Jonah and the whale is read. God asked Jonah to visit some bad people and make them good. But Jonah wanted them punished, so he ignored God and ran away to sea.

While he was at sea, Jonah was swallowed by a whale. Inside the whale, he prayed to God for forgiveness for disobeying him, and God saved him. This story tells people they cannot run away from the bad things they have done and that, if they say sorry, God will forgive them.

This old wall painting from Turkey shows Jonah after three days, when the whale spit him out on to dry land.

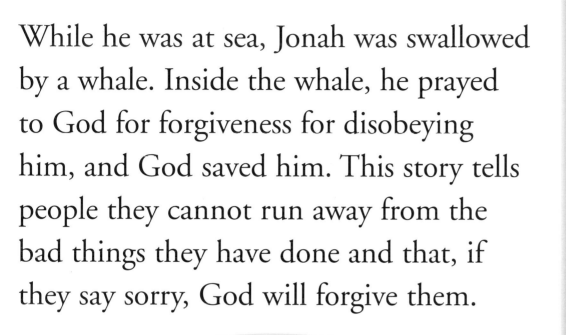

17

All is forgiven

The doors of the Ark are open to show that the gates of heaven are open when prayers are said.

The synagogue services begin in the morning. Then there is a short break, and the afternoon and evening prayers are said.

DID YOU KNOW?

The Ark is a special cupboard in the synagogue where the holy Torah scrolls are kept.

18

The final prayer is called the Ne'ilah, which is only said on the day of Yom Kippur. Jews hope that God will forgive them as they stand and say prayers, and then hear the shofar, or ram's horn.

The long shofar note, which is blown in all synagogues, at the end of Yom Kippur, is the final call for forgiveness.

19

Fasting

Jews are not supposed to go to school or work on Yom Kippur.

On the day of Yom Kippur, many Jews fast for 25 hours. This means that no one can drink or eat anything. This is so that people can pray and think about God, without having to worry about food. Children under the age of 13 and people who are sick do not have to fast.

On this day, people are not allowed to have a bath, wear perfume or makeup, or wear leather shoes.

This sign says, "Fabric shoes for Yom Kippur." Leather shoes must not be worn since they are a **luxury**.

DID YOU KNOW?

In Israel, on Yom Kippur there are no radio or television programs.

21

The festival of bicycles

In Israel, Yom Kippur is also called the "festival of bicycles." Israel is a Jewish country, so most Jews do not drive their cars during Yom Kippur.

During Yom Kippur, people in Israel walk and cycle along the wide roads.

Children play safely on the streets in Israel on Yom Kippur, since there is no traffic.

Children enjoy riding their bicycles on the empty roads. They also go roller-skating and skateboarding.

Index and further information

GLOSSARY

ancient a very long time ago

blessing to ask God to look after someone

fast to go without food or beverages

luxury something that costs a lot of money and that you don't really need

prophet someone who teaches the word of God on Earth

rabbi a Jewish religious leader

Rosh Hashanah the Jewish New Year

traditional something passed down from generation to generation

worship to show love and respect to God

BOOKS TO READ

Judaism (Religions of the World) by Michael Keene (World Almanac Library, 2006)

Rosh Hashanah and Yom Kippur by Dana Meachen Rau (Topeka Bindery, 2004)